MW01244563

THE PROFESSIONAL MINDSET

ALSO BY STEVEN PRESSFIELD

FICTION

The Legend of Bagger Vance
Gates of Fire
Tides of War
Last of the Amazons
The Virtues of War
The Afghan Campaign
Killing Rommel
The Profession
The Knowledge
36 Righteous Men (2019)

NONFICTION

The War of Art
The Warrior Ethos
Turning Pro
The Authentic Swing
Do the Work
The Lion's Gate
An American Jew
Nobody Wants to Read Your Sh*t
The Artist's Journey

THE PROFESSIONAL MINDSET

Notes on Mental Toughness for
Writers and Artists

STEVEN PRESSFIELD

A BLACK IRISH JAB
BLACK IRISH ENTERTAINMENT LLC

Black Irish Entertainment LLC
223 Egremont Plain Road
PMB 191
Egremont, MA 01230
Copyright (c) 2018 by Steven Pressfield
Cover Design by Derick Tsai, Magnus Rex
Interior Design by Spring Hoteling

All Rights Reserved

First Black Irish Entertainment Paperback Edition

March 2019

For Information About Special Discounts
for Bulk Purchases,
Please Visit www.blackirishbooks.com
ISBN: 978-1-936891-46-7
Ebook: 978-1-936891-64-1

"I will expect no opportunity until I have first created value for someone else."

> — **Dan Sullivan** of Strategic Coach, on the promise an entrepreneur makes to herself when she embarks upon her entrepreneurial career.

A NOTE TO THE READER

Unedited drafts of some of the materials within were first published as part of the "Writing Wednesdays" column on www.stevenpressfield.com.

About Black Irish Jabs

In the heat of battle against Resistance, when you're on the ropes and your guard begins to fall, you don't need a five-hundred-page treatise on the whys and wherefores of syntax or global story structure.

You need a shot of adrenaline to quickly remind you of storytelling's first principles.

That's what Black Irish Jabs are—short, laser-targeted and to the point pieces of professional craft advice to put Resistance where it belongs . . . back on its heels.

Now get back in the ring!

—Steven Pressfield and Shawn Coyne

1
WRITER = ENTREPRENEUR

Are you a writer? A filmmaker? A dancer?

Then you're an entrepreneur.

You have more in common with Steve Jobs and Elon Musk than you do with your dad who worked all his life for General Motors or your aunt who's five months away from collecting her pension from the Post Office.

Consider the character of the artist and the entrepreneur.

What emotional and psychological qualities does a writer need in order to conceive a project, to initiate it in the face of her own self-doubt and the indifference (and often outright hostility) of others, to hang tough through the "second act horrors," to bring the work to completion, and then take it to market in the cold, cruel world?

Aren't these the same qualities that Jeff Bezos or Sergey Brin or Mark Zuckerberg needed to launch and bring to success Amazon or Google or Facebook?

How should she think of herself, this writer or artist? What is her most effective self-conception?

Step One, it seems to me, is to recognize that all of us—writers, artists, filmmakers, actors, musicians—are entrepreneurs.

We don't work for the Man.

We work for ourselves.

We don't look to a boss, an authority figure, or an organization for daily structure, for validation of worth, for monetary support. We look to ourselves.

What is an entrepreneur anyway?

My online dictionary says the word comes from the French, *entreprende*, "to undertake." It's related to "enterprise."

> A person who sets up a business or businesses, taking on financial risks in the hope of profit.

Dan Sullivan of Strategic Coach defines an entrepreneur as

> Someone who has an exceptionally personal relationship with the first of the month.

Meaning payday.

The artist, if you think about it, is the ultimate entrepreneur.

She is in business entirely for herself.

She has no boss.

She gets no paycheck, except from herself.

She has no imposed daily schedule.

No externally imposed structure.

No one pats her on the back.

No one mentors her or critiques her, unless she finds that mentor herself.

No one rewards her.

The artist (the writer, the actor, the composer, the videogame designer) possesses total workplace freedom. She can tackle any project she wants, execute it any way she wishes, take it to market any way she desires.

She can write a novel, audition for a Broadway play, compose a symphony, lay out the next *Assassin's Creed*.

That's Jobs and Wozniak in the early seventies.

That's Bill Gates and Warren Buffett and Larry Page.

It's also X million other dudes that you and I have never heard of.

The thing about being an entrepreneur is you can go all the way up ... or all the way down. Nothing is stopping you from either outcome. Nothing except yourself.

In the succeeding chapters we're going to examine what it takes, emotionally and psychologically, to succeed in the entrepreneurial universe.

We're going to take a hard look at the Professional Mindset and how it applies to those of us seeking to make our living/satisfy our soul at the intersection of Art and Commerce.

2
TK THIS JOB N SHOVE IT

When you and I were working on the assembly line at Ford in Dearborn, we had to worry about our production quotas, our standards of workmanship, our supervisor's evaluations of us.

What we *didn't* have to worry about was the structure of our day.

That structure was imposed upon us from outside.

Then one day we quit.

Suddenly we were artists.

We were entrepreneurs.

We thought it would be easy. We were free! Nothing could stop us!

It turned out to be the hardest thing we'd ever done.

Suddenly, like Dorothy swept up from Kansas or Luke following Obi-Wan Kenobi, we had embarked upon our own Hero's Journey. We had left the Ordinary World and entered the Inverted World, the Extraordinary World.

In this new world, all things became possible. Our life could change. Our future could change. Our prospects could change.

There was only one problem: *we ourselves had to change.*

We could not survive in the Extraordinary World using the mindset that had worked for us in the Ordinary World.

How exactly did we have to change?

We had to make the mental shift from externally imposed discipline to *self-discipline*.

This, in one sentence, is the difference between the laborer-for-hire and the entrepreneur.

This is the Professional Mindset.

I begin each day of my life with a ritual. I wake up at 5:30 a.m., put on my workout clothes, my leg-warmers, my sweatshirts, and my hat. I walk outside my Manhattan home, hail a taxi, and tell the driver to take me to the Pumping Iron gym at 91st Street and First Avenue, where I work out for two hours [before heading to my dance studio to begin the day's work]. The ritual is not the stretching and weight training I put my body through each morning at the gym; the ritual is the cab. The moment I tell the driver where to go I have completed my ritual.

Do you see the Professional Mindset in this passage from Twyla Tharp's *The Creative Habit*?

I've quoted these paragraphs before, and I'm sure I'll cite them again and again because they so eloquently articulate the Mindset of the Artist.

Encapsulated within Ms. Tharp's morning ritual are virtually all the qualities of mental toughness that the artist/entrepreneur needs:

Self-motivation.

Self-discipline.

Self-reinforcement.

Self-validation.

Self-belief.

And they're all wrapped up in the artist/entrepreneur's secret package: habit.

When you and I worked on the line at Dearborn, we didn't need the Professional Mindset. Ford supplied that for us.

Ford told us when to wake up.

It told us when to show up for work.

Ford told us what we could wear and what we could not wear.

It told us how many hours we had to stay on the job, how many days a week, how many months a year.

Ford told us when we could go to lunch.

When we could take a vacation.

When we could leave the line to heed nature's call.

Ford even supplied a factory whistle to tell us when the day was over and we could go home.

We were not amateurs at Ford. We were professionals. But we were professionals whose professionalism was *imposed upon us from outside*, under penalty of disciplinary action, penalty of fine, penalty of termination.

There's nothing wrong with any of the rules or strictures that Ford or any other company imposes on its employees. If you and I were running a similar enterprise, we'd make our workers do exactly the same. It's how good cars get made. It's how professional work gets done. It's how a business survives and prospers.

What exactly, we might then ask, is the Professional Mindset ... the mindset of the individual who has left the factory and has set herself up as an artist and an entrepreneur on her own?

What should she do differently from when she worked on the line?

> Answer: We do exactly what we did when we were working for Ford, only instead of Ford telling us what to do, *we tell ourselves.*

Instead of Ford setting the agenda, we set it.

We decide what our goal is—and how we intend to reach it.

We decide how much we're willing to sacrifice to reach that goal.

We decide how many hours we will work (our total, bank on it, will be MUCH HIGHER than it was at Ford) and how many weeks and months per year.

We decide where we will work.

We decide when.

And with whom.

We decide what time we get up and what time we go to bed. We assign our own vacations and our own days off. We also assign all-nighters and working weekends.

We alone will be the arbiters of our success.

We'll give ourselves a raise if and when we deserve it.

And we'll kick ourselves in the butt when we screw up.

We will be our own boss, our own employer, our own mentor and teacher and psychiatrist.

Can we do that?

Can we make that mental shift?

Can we flip that switch in our mind?

If our goal is to be a writer or an artist or an entrepreneur, we can't do it any other way.

3
YOU, INC.

If an artist is an entrepreneur (and she is), then she too must navigate this passage from externally-imposed structure to self-imposed structure.

She must move from external discipline to self-discipline. From external validation to self-validation. From external reinforcement to self-reinforcement.

In a way, she is like a nation that declares its independence.

She has sued for the right to self-determination and she has won.

Now what?

What *is* self-determination?

How do we enact it? How do we produce it in ourselves?

Think it's easy? Ask yourself, of the new world you think to enter:

> What time will I get up in the morning?
> What will I eat for breakfast?
> What thoughts will I permit myself to indulge in over breakfast?
> Where will I go when I finish my meal?

What will I do once I get there?

What will I do when I encounter my own internal Resistance?

How do I answer the voice in my head that tells me I'm worthless, that my dreams are folly, that I've made a terrible mistake leaving that job at Ford?

How do I respond to external adversity? To real-world competition? To my own flawed business judgment? To the bottom dropping out of the marketplace?

What happens when my rent doubles?

When my permits expire?

How do I placate my worried spouse, my anxious children? What do I tell them when I myself am more freaked out than they are?

How do I handle failure?

How do I keep going?

How do I keep from losing my mind?

The Professional Mindset is not taught in high school and it's not taught in college. They don't school you in it at Harvard and they don't teach it to you at the Iowa Writers' Workshop.

Your education begins, unfortunately, the day you tell your boss to take this job and shove it, or your spouse dies or walks out on you, or you're discharged from the army, or your knees give out as a professional athlete. You enter this new world when you're fired, or you quit, or the plant closes or the business moves to Mexico.

It's scary.

It's like one of those survivor shows on TV. They drop you out of an airplane into the Amazon jungle. Good luck, sucker!

You're on your own.

4
YOU, INC., PART TWO

I had a friend when I worked in Hollywood named Victoria. Victoria was a star screenwriter. One day she took me out to lunch and gave me some advice about handling oneself in "this town."

> Steve, every day you and I go up against Twentieth-Century Fox and Warner Bros. and Paramount. They're our competition. We've got to be just as organized as they are, just as tough, and just as smart.

Victoria told me how she organized herself as a writer/entrepreneur.

> Fox has a slate of pictures in development, right? I've got one too. Warners has a five-year plan. I've got one too. Everything the studios do, I do. I'm not just as organized, I'm more organized.

I immediately adopted Victoria's business model.

If you've ever worked in a corporation, you know about Monday morning status meetings. The group assembles in the conference room or the boss's office. Plans are discussed. Assignments are given out. The boss's secretary types up an Action List and distributes it. Now every team member knows where every ongoing project stands and what action is required of him or her for the coming week.

I adopted that plan exactly.

I still work that way.

Every Monday morning I have a meeting with myself. I go over everything I've got to do. I assign myself tasks and set myself goals and deadlines. I type up an Action List and distribute it to myself. If I succeed through the week, I reward myself. If I screw up, I kick myself in the ass.

The Professional Mindset begins with a radical reconceptualization of ourselves as artists and as entrepreneurs.

When we adopt the Professional Mindset, we stop thinking of ourselves as individuals (with all the flaws, fears, and weaknesses that every individual inevitably possesses).

We start thinking of ourselves as an enterprise.

After I'd been in Hollywood for a few years, I realized that many writers worked as one-man corporations. They did not hire themselves out as themselves but f/s/o ("for services of") themselves as writers.

I had never heard of this before. I thought it was pretty cool.

I formed my own corporation the minute I could afford it.

13

Why did this idea appeal to me? Not just for the tax benefits or the advantages involving medical insurance (though those were a factor, I admit).

I loved the psychology.

If I think of myself as Me, Inc., I'm no longer so alone in the world.

I've stopped being a fragile, vulnerable individual. I'm now an entity, like Apple or Facebook or General Dynamics.

I'm an operation.

I'm an enterprise.

As Cary Grant (as Sgt. Archibald Cutter) declared to Victor McLaglen (as Sgt. "Mac" MacChesney) in *Gunga Din* as he set out to find the temple of gold:

SGT. CUTTER
You're not looking at a soldier, MacChesney. You're looking at an expedition! Stand aside! Make way for the expedition!

Remember, our enemy as writers is not other writers, or lazy agents, or the marketplace, or the slings and arrows of Amazon.

The enemy is Resistance.

The enemy is our own internal self-sabotage.

Thinking of myself as a corporation (or an expedition) gave me a weapon against Resistance.

I could no longer say to myself (or, more accurately, allow my own Resistance to bray at me), "Steve, you're a loser. That last piece of work was garbage, and you're gonna follow it up with more garbage, etc."

Now I say to myself, "Okay, we suffered a bit of a setback. Perhaps our instincts were not as spot-on as we had thought. Let's schedule a meeting with our self to regroup and decide on next steps."

I'm a corporation.

I may still be myself-the-writer, but I'm also myself-the-CEO-of-the-corporation. Under pressure, the writer may panic. He may become overwhelmed with self-doubt and fall prey to impulses of self-destruction. But the CEO maintains his own cool. He holds in mind the Big Picture. He'll send the writer to Palm Springs for a three-day vacation if he thinks that'll get him back to his old self. Or he'll put him up against the wall and read him the Riot Act.

Either way, I/me/my company are operating at the same professional level as the corporations we are competing against. We are the Google and the Facebook and the Tesla of our own mind.

Those Fortune 500 corporations are not going to falter and neither are we. We're as self-energized as they are, as self-organized, and as self-sustaining. There is nothing they can do in their sphere that we can't do in ours.

SGT. CUTTER

Stand back, MacChesney! Make way for the expedition!

5
FRANK SINATRA DOES NOT MOVE PIANOS

I've quoted Dan Sullivan and I'm gonna do it again. Do you know him? He's the founder and CEO of Strategic Coach and one of the great mentors to entrepreneurs in the world. So, in keeping with these chapters on the Professional Mindset, let me rip off a few more of his ideas for you. (Thanks, Dan!)

Dan tells the story that when he was in the army stationed in Korea, one of his jobs was putting together shows for the troops. Frank Sinatra came over one time. Dan studied him carefully and, as he says,

> One of the things I learned was that Frank Sinatra does not move pianos.

Frank has other guys to do that. Frank does only two things, Dan says.

> Frank Sinatra sings, and he prepares to sing. That's it.

Dan Sullivan has a concept he calls "Unique Ability." Unique ability, Dan explains, is the individual entrepreneur's one-of-a-kind gift. It's her singular talent, the one thing she brings to her business that nobody else can bring.

Steve Jobs had a unique ability.

Seth Godin has it.

Shawn Coyne has it.

You have it too. In many ways your job as a writer or an artist is to identify your unique ability and then organize your day, your month, and your year in such a way that you maximize your time exercising your unique ability and minimize or outsource everything else.

When I was in Israel researching *The Lion's Gate*, I interviewed a number of people who had been close to Moshe Dayan, the great Israeli general and Minister of Defense. I heard over and over that Dayan used to say, "I don't want to do anything that somebody else can do."

In other words, Dayan brought something unique to the table. No doubt this quality was hard to define. It was intangible. Vision, perhaps. Charisma. Whatever it was, Dayan understood it and so did everyone around him.

His soldiers did not want Moshe Dayan to move pianos. If he had tried to move a piano, his officers would have tackled him and dragged him off the stage. They wanted Dayan to command, to do what he could do that nobody else could do.

Dan Sullivan, when he speaks of unique ability, is not thinking specifically of writers or artists. He's thinking of entrepreneurs. He's thinking of Larry Ellison or Sergey Brin or Steve Jobs. But the concept applies, I believe, more to writers and artists than to anybody.

Stephen King has unique ability.

So does Toni Morrison.

And Tom Wolfe and Harper Lee and J.D. Salinger.

Each of them brings something to the party that nobody else can bring.

I read somewhere that we all should find that one thing that we can do better than anyone else in the world. When I first heard that, I thought, "That's a bit grandiose, isn't it? What could we possibly do that fifty thousand other people couldn't do better?"

I was wrong.

I have something, maybe more than one thing, that I can do better than anyone else in the world. So does my friend Randy and my friend Victoria. So do you.

My friend Mike just showed me a manuscript he's been working on for five years. The pile of pages was a foot high. Mike's book had created an entire world, down to the most minute details. He was, in the arena he had envisioned and brought to life, the best in the world.

He was Frank Sinatra.

As writers and artists, our unique ability is our voice. Our peculiar, idiosyncratic point of view. Our sense of humor, our sense of irony, our one of a kind vision of the world.

Don't feel bad if you're twenty years old or forty years old and you're saying to yourself, "I don't know what my unique voice is."

The truth is we don't know what our voice is until we sing once, and sing again, and sing again and again.

I've said before that I had no idea what books would come out of me until they came, and when they did, I was more surprised by them than anybody.

Our voice is there already.

We were born with it.

Our Muse knows it, even if we (so far) don't.

We reveal it to ourselves and to the world through work. By following our creative heart and seeing what comes out.

The Professional Mindset is about NOT moving pianos. It's about finding that unique voice that is ours alone.

Frank Sinatra sings, and he prepares to sing.

That's it.

6
YOUR RESISTANCE AND MINE

Here we are, five chapters into our investigation of the Professional Mindset. Let's pause here and return to Square One:

What is the Professional Mindset about?

Why do we even need it? Can't we just cruise through on instinct and our good looks?

Why do we have to work so hard and be so organized? Can't we just be happy amateurs?

What is the Professional Mindset about anyway?

The Professional Mindset is about Resistance.

We adopt the Professional Mindset for one reason only: to combat our own internal self-sabotage.

The professional mindset is a weapon against Resistance, like AA is a weapon against alcoholism.

Don't laugh. The analogy is exact.

Have you, the writer, ever woken up metaphorically face-down in the gutter at five in the morning with an empty bottle beside you?

I have.

Have you ever said to yourself, "I am powerless against this force that is destroying me from inside"?

I have.

Have you ever said to yourself, "I don't know how I'm going to do it, but I'm going to turn my life around, starting right here and right now"?

Some people might call that moment "hitting bottom."

I call it "turning pro."

I call it switching to the Professional Mindset.

In Twelve Step programs the first action you take is to admit you are beaten. You acknowledge that a certain internally generated negative force has power over you. It has defeated you over and over, and it is going to destroy you completely if you can't get a handle on facing it and containing it.

As writers and artists, we wake up with that negative force every morning.

Resistance never goes away.

It never gets any easier.

We are exactly like recovering alcoholics.

Our booze is Resistance.

It tempts us every day, every hour. It's seductive, it's diabolical, it's indefatigable.

In Twelve Step programs, the individual's mantra is "One Day at a Time."

That's our mantra too.

I don't go to meetings like individuals in AA or Al-Anon or other Twelve Step programs.

These chapters are my meetings.

I reinforce myself with them. I screw up my courage by sharing my losses and victories on the page, on the web.

The principles involved are the same.

Humility.

Acceptance of vulnerability.

Resolve to prevail.

The Professional Mindset, in whatever form you or I adopt it, is the most powerful weapon I know of in the battle against Resistance and self-sabotage.

We spoke a couple of chapters ago about "You, Inc." In other words, the idea of thinking of ourselves not as vulnerable individuals but as highly charged enterprises.

You, Inc. is a mind trick. It's a head game. But it works, just like Twelve Step programs work.

To think of ourselves as professionals (as opposed to amateurs) eliminates self-judgment and self-condemnation, both of which are weapons that our own Resistance uses against us.

There's nothing wrong with you if you wake up every morning with that dragon in your head.

Sappho woke up that way.

Dostoevsky woke up that way.

Shakespeare woke up that way.

They all experienced a moment when they said to themselves, "I accept this as my internal reality. From this day forward, I will organize my inner resources not to yield to this negative force but to face it and overcome it."

Repeat after me:

"My name is _____ and I have been defeated by Resistance."

Now we can begin.

7
WARRIORS AND MOTHERS

What are the virtues of an entrepreneur?

What qualities of mind do you and I need if we are going to succeed as artists/entrepreneurs?

One answer (the one I usually use) is to say we need the virtues of warriors:

Courage.

Patience.

Self-reliance.

The ability to endure adversity.

Another way (which is even better) is to say we need the virtues of mothers.

I had a dream once. It came like this. I was living in New York, driving a cab at night, trying to write in the daytime. A friend came to visit. (This is the real-life setup, not the dream.) My friend was one of these wildly extroverted guys, who immediately went out on the town and came back with fabulous stories of all the fun he was having. I found myself thinking, *I should be like him. Why am I denying myself everything, busting my butt day and night? Have fun, Steve! Stop being such a monk!*

Then I had the dream. In the dream another friend's wife, who happened to be pregnant at that time, came to me and sat down at my kitchen table. "Steve, you are pregnant too," she said, "with that book you're writing. You can't go out partying. Your responsibility is to the new life growing inside you."

The dream was right.

I woke up and immediately stopped worrying.

That movie that's gestating inside you? That's your baby.

That novel.

That album.

That new business.

The virtues you and I need to develop are the virtues of mothers.

A mother puts her own needs second (or third or fourth or fifth). The needs of her child come first.

A mother will kill to protect her baby.

She will sacrifice her own life.

She'll run into a burning building to save her child.

She'll lift a Buick off her infant with her bare hands.

A mother knows how to say no.

No, she won't go to the club.

No, she won't drink those mojitos.

No, she won't ingest that banned substance.

A mother eats right.

A mother gets her sleep.

A mother weans herself off Facebook and Twitter and Pinterest and Instagram (at least most of the time).

A mother is the definition of tough-minded.

A mother is the consummate professional.

She is in it for keeps.

She is in it for the long haul.

She is in it 24/7/365.

Nothing under the sun can shake a mother from her object, which is to nurture and protect and defend and prepare her baby to grow into its fullest possible potential.

A warrior is nothing compared to a mother.

Wanna be an artist? An entrepreneur?

Be a mother.

8
YOUR CORPORATE CULTURE

Let's flash back to chapters 3 and 4, the "You, Inc." chapters.

I remarked in those pages that many Hollywood screenwriters (including me) find it useful to incorporate themselves.

These writers don't perform their labors as themselves but as "loan-outs" from their one-man or one-woman corporations. Their contracts are "f/s/o"—for services of—themselves.

I'm a big fan of this way of operating. Not just for the financial or legal benefits, but for the mindset this style of working promotes.

If you and I are a corporation, we've gotta get our act together.

Amateur hour is over for us.

If we're competing (and we are) against Google and Apple and Twentieth-Century Fox, we've got to be as focused and as organized as they are. We need a vision for our enterprise. We need discipline. We need dedication. We need tenacity.

In other words, we need a culture.

Apple has a culture. Steve Jobs inculcated it.

The New England Patriots have a culture. It came from Bill Belichick and Robert Kraft and Tom Brady.

What's your culture?

Twyla Tharp's got one.

I don't know exactly what Stephen King's work habits are, but I know he's there at his keyboard 365 days a year, including Christmas and his birthday.

That's Stephen King's culture.

A culture performs a number of functions for people like you and me.

One, it establishes a level of effort.

How hard do we imagine Steve Jobs worked? Michael Jordan? Derek Jeter?

A culture establishes a standard of performance below which we within the culture will not let ourselves fall.

At what level of performance does Toni Morrison operate?

A culture lays out standards of ethics.

What degree of moral chicanery will Seth Godin tolerate?

But most of all a culture gives us a vision for the future, for our future.

When a new coach is hired for an athletic team or a new CEO comes on board at a company, his or her primary objective is to establish a winning mindset.

She banishes laziness and tentativeness. She elevates the level of commitment. She gets her players to buy in to a vision whose object is to produce victory (or success), if not immediately then over time.

A culture establishes a style—a way of working that best expresses our natural bent and gives us the best chance to be who we are and to produce the stuff that is most uniquely our own. At IBM in the fifties that meant white shirts and black ties. At Facebook today it's T-shirts and sneakers (at least I think it is; I've never been inside Facebook).

What's Rihanna's style?

What's yours?

The difference between an amateur and a professional is an amateur has an amateur culture and a professional has a professional culture.

What's yours?

9
POLITICS AND THE PROFESSIONAL MINDSET

Candidates for office in all lands and in every century make the same promise to the voters they hope to attract:

> I will get you what you want and it will cost you nothing.

Want your job back? A free college education? No problem. I'll get it for you.

Something for nothing is the offer a drug dealer makes to an addict or a mother provides for an infant.

In the grownup world, something for nothing does not exist. Yet politicians sell it to us, and we fall for it every time. Why?

The amateur, the infant, and the addict operate out of the identical mindset. Each looks to others—specifically others perceived to be more powerful or capable—to supply their needs or solve their problems.

> I will get you what you want and it will cost you nothing.

The candidate for office adds two particularly perverse corollaries to this proposal.

The straits in which you find yourself are not your fault. You are blameless. You were duped and betrayed by (insert Vulnerable Minority here), upon whom you shall now, by my agency, wreak your vengeance.

And

You need pay nothing for the solution to your problem. We will take the money from (insert Affluent Minority here.)

Why am I bringing this up? It's not a rant, really. My aim is to contrast the amateur/addict/infant mindset to the mindset of the professional—whether she be an artist, an entrepreneur, a mother, a student, whatever.

The professional starts from the following assumption (I'm borrowing from Dan Sullivan of Strategic Coach here):

I will expect no opportunity and no remuneration until I have first created value for someone else.

I was watching a terrific PBS "American Masters" documentary about David Geffen, who rose from humble beginnings (in Brooklyn, natch) to become a legend in the entertainment biz and a renowned philanthropist. When he was a boy, David was offered the following piece of wisdom by his mother:

You'd better learn to like to work, because we have no money and you're going to be working for the rest of your life.

Another authority figure once made a similar statement to a pair of innocents under His care:

And unto Adam he said, Because thou hast hearkened unto the voice of thy wife, and hast eaten of the tree, of which I commanded thee, saying, Thou shalt not eat of it: cursed is the ground for thy sake; in sorrow shalt thou eat of it all the days of thy life; Thorns also and thistles shall it bring forth to thee; and thou shalt eat the herb of the field; In the sweat of thy face shalt thou eat bread, till thou return unto the ground; for out of it wast thou taken: for dust thou art, and unto dust shalt thou return.

The professional is immune to politician-type promises, whether they come to her from outside or from within her own head. She recognizes them for what they are.

Instead she tells herself, *Whatever I want, whatsoever problems confront me and my family, no one is going to solve them but me. The only way I (or anyone) will change my circumstances for the better is through good sense and hard work.*

The professional mindset is hard-core. Why? Because it reflects the realities of life.

How do you write a novel?

How do you make a movie?

How do you raise a child?

The only time life is not hard-core is when it is portrayed in the speeches of candidates campaigning for office.

By the way, whatever happened to

"Ask not what your country can do for you, ask what you can do for your country"?

Not to mention

"I have nothing to offer but blood, toil, tears and sweat."

Maybe I am ranting. The point I'm trying to make is that JFK and Winston Churchill in those phrases addressed their constituents as if they were adults and as if they possessed the professional mindset.

10
SURVIVING IN THE DESERT

A few years ago I wrote a book called *Killing Rommel*. *Killing Rommel* is a novel set during WWII in the North Africa campaign. Its heroes are the men of the Long Range Desert Group, a true historical British commando unit that fought behind the lines against Field Marshal Erwin Rommel and the German Afrika Korps.

The first time I heard the name Long Range Desert Group, I fell in love with it. I said to myself, "I don't know what this is, but I gotta write a book about it."

"Long Range." So much cooler that Short Range.

Even better: "Long Range Desert." Somebody was going out into the Tall Sand a long, long way.

And "Long Range Desert Group?" It didn't sound typically military. It sounded like a tech start-up.

The LRDG, it turned out, smacked more of a civilian outfit than an over-organized, rigorously disciplined military team. The trucks they drove into the desert were Chevy "30-hundredweights" bought from civvie dealerships in Cairo. Discipline was slack. Improvisation was the order of the day.

Why did I love this subject?

Because it reminded me of the writer's life.

The men of the LRDG had a mission. Their charge was to leave civilization behind and advance alone into the unknown. Once out there, they could call on no one for aid or rescue. They were on their own, with nothing to assure their success except that which they brought with them.

That's you and me.

That's the writer's life.

The desert is a metaphor for the creative sphere that you and I operate in. The desert is beautiful. It's remote, it's odd, it's strange. Only a special few dare to enter.

The desert contains secrets. It's mysterious; it seems barren but it's actually teeming with life if you know where to look.

The desert is reality stripped to its essentials. It's pure. It's geometric. Its landscape has been shaped by nothing but the elemental forces of wind, water, and time.

The desert is cruel. It will cook you, freeze you, drown you. Worse, the desert is indifferent. It doesn't care if you live or die. Its sand will drift over your corpse in minutes. It will forget you as if you never existed.

That's our world, yours and mine. It's the dimension we enter every day, seeking our Muse.

What about enemies?

The desert holds two—the external foe (in the case of the Long Range Desert Group, the enemy was the Afrika Korps) and the internal adversary, the men's own fears and Resistance.

Think about it. Your truck breaks down five hundred miles from civilization. (Forget the Afrika Korps for the moment; we're dealing now with pure survival.) By noon, external temperature will hit 130 Fahrenheit. Can you keep your head? Can you improvise a fix for your cracked engine block? Can you stretch twenty gallons of fuel to carry you home?

That's you and me at page 183 in our novel. That's us in the middle at Act Two.

What I love too about the Long Range Desert Group is that it was—and had to be, by the nature of its mission and grounds upon which it operated—self-contained.

Into the beds of those Chevy trucks the men of the LRDG loaded fuel, water, rations, radio gear, weapons, ammunition, spare parts. Into nooks and crannies they wedged their bedding and clothing, their tea and tins of bully beef. Like sailors they brought rum, in porcelain demijohn jars labeled S.R.D. (for Service Reserve Depot) that they translated as "Seldom Reaches Destination."

That's you and me too. The essence of our artistic/ entrepreneurial life is that it is and must be self-contained.

We and we alone must decide what we will work on, and how, for how long, under what conditions, with what ambitions and aspirations. We have to master the art of self-evaluation. Is our idea good? Good enough to give two years or more of our lives to?

When our vehicle founders in the Sand Sea, what resources can we call on within ourselves? The cavalry isn't coming. It's up to us and us alone.

One of the most interesting aspects of the Long Range Desert Group was the type of men it sought for its ranks.

The LRDG never lacked for volunteers. Out of one application-round of eight hundred men, it selected twelve.

Most of the men in the Long Range Desert Group were Kiwis. New Zealanders. They were farmers and stockmen, mechanics and farm appraisers. Their age was roughly ten years older than regular line troops. Most were married and had children. No few owned and worked farms and ranches of considerable size.

They were mature men (alas, no women went into the desert in that era, though that almost certainly would be different today) whose primary emotional characteristics were resourcefulness, level-headedness, self-composure, patience, the ability to work well in close quarters with others, the capacity to endure adversity and even to thrive on it, and, not least, the possession of a sense of humor.

In other words they weren't blood-and-guts man-killers. (Okay, some were.) They were cool customers, possessed of grit and savvy, who could embark on a mission whose hazard was such that saner heads would call it absolutely nuts—and see that mission through, no matter what.

Isn't it interesting that those are the same qualities you and I need as writers and artists to survive and even thrive in our own inner deserts?

ABOUT THE AUTHOR

STEVEN PRESSFIELD is the bestselling author of *The Legend of Bagger Vance, Gates of Fire, The Afghan Campaign,* and *The Lion's Gate,* as well as the cult classics on creativity, *The War of Art, Turning Pro, Do the Work,* and *Nobody Wants to Read Your Sh*t.*

His Wednesday column on www.StevenPressfield.com is among the most popular writing blogs on the web.

facebook.com/StevePressfield

twitter.com/spressfield